CREATIVE K
YUM!-SCHOOLING
COOKBOOK

15 STEP-BY STEP RECIPES
with coloring and activities

Katya Brown

illustrator: Tolik Trishkin

published by Sarah Janisse Brown and
The Thinking Tree LLC
www.funschoolingbooks.com
copyright 2017

TABLE OF CONTENTS:

HOW TO USE THIS BOOK:

This is a cookbook, but it is also so much more. Little ones can learn the joy of baking together with an adult, and bigger kids can try simple recipes on their own or with the help of someone older. Teens can immerse themselves in the recipes and perfect their skills.

You can decide their level of skill and responsibility, while helping them pick the recipe that is just right for them.

But more than just a primer on beloved classics and innovative recipes alike; It is also a coloring book, a journal full of activities, and an access point for imagination. There are fun facts, puzzles, quizzes, and more. there is even space to change recipes or create new once from scratch.

This book is perfect for home-schooling, car rides, visits to Grandma, or just the joy of learning a new skill.

We hope you enjoy using this book as much as we enjoyed making it, because we found it yummy!

- Katya Brown

BEST BANANA BREAD

INGREDIENTS:

3 bananas (the browner the better)
1/3 cup butter
1/2- 1cup sugar
(amount depends on how sweet you want it)
1 egg
1 teaspoon vanilla extract
1 teaspoon baking soda
Pinch of salt
1 1/2 cups flour

3 bananas (the browner the better)

1/3 cup butter

1/2- 1cup sugar

1 teaspoon baking soda

1 teaspoon
vanilla extract

Pinch of salt

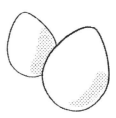

1 egg

1 1/2 cups flour

TOOLS:

Oven
Standard loaf pan (9x5x3)
Wax paper
Big bowl
Whisk
Fork
Spatula
Measuring cups
Measuring spoons
Oven mitts
Cooling rack
Toothpick

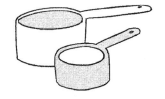

Measuring cups

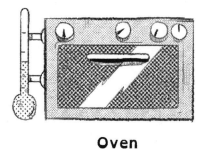

Oven

Spatula

Cooling rack

loaf pan

Toothpick

Fork

Big bowl

Wax paper

Whisk

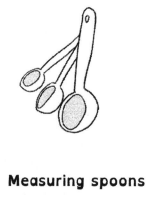

Measuring spoons

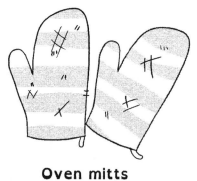

Oven mitts

INSTRUCTIONS

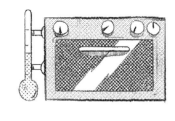

Step 1: Preheat oven to 350
and line loaf pan with wax paper.

Step 2: melt butter and mash bananas with fork,
and whisk egg.

Step3: In the bowl,
mix all ingredients by with fork or whisk
until even and smooth.

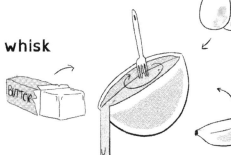

For
50 min

Step4: Pour   into a lined loaf pan

Step 5: Bake 50 minutes or until browned.
Insert toothpick in middle of bread.
If it comes out clean, it is done.

CLEAN

Step 6: Cool on rack. Slice,
and enjoy the "Best Banana Bread" ever.

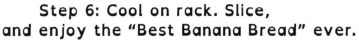

MY RECIPE CHECKLIST

- ☐ Do I have all the ingredients
- ☐ Do I have all the tools
- ☐ Do I have permission
- ☐ Do I have a clock to watch the time
- ☐ Am I following all safety rules
- ☐ Have I followed all instructions
- ☐ Have I turned off all equipment
- ☐ Have I cleaned everything up
- ☐ Have I tasted it?

DRAW A PICTURE THE RECIPE,
YOUR RESULTS,
SOMETHING FUN ABOUT THE PROCESS,
OR SOMEONE EATING IT!

QUESTIONS & ANSWERS

HOW DID YOU LIKE THIS RECIPE?

HOW DID IT TASTE?

WHAT WAS DIFFICULT ABOUT MAKING IT?

WHAT DO YOU THINK COULD MAKE THIS RECIPE BETTER?

DID YOU LEARN ANYTHING NEW?

WHO DO YOU KNOW THAT WOULD LIKE THIS TREAT?

You have just finished baking your first recipe. **I hope you enjoyed it.**
Early American settlers had the philosophy:
If you won't work, you don't get to eat.
This was a principle they found in the Bible (2 Thessalonians 3:10).
It feels good to work with your hands.
It feels even better to enjoy the yummy results of that work.
I hope you have a better appreciation of everyone that cooks,
cleans, and cares for you.

What are some things that others do for you? Do you appreciate it?

- -

- -

- -

How do you feel about eating the reward of your hard work?

- -

- -

- -

How does it feel to see others enjoying what you do?

- -

- -

- -

What are some other things you can start doing for yourself

- -

- -

- -

How can you show gratitude for those that work hard for you?

- -

- -

- -

BASIC-DELICIOUS BROWNIES

INGREDIENTS:

1/2 cup butter
1 1/2 cups sugar
1/2 teaspoon vanilla extract
2 eggs
3/4 cup flour
1/2 cup cocoa powder
1/4 teaspoon salt
1/4 teaspoon baking soda
1 cup dark (semi sweet) chocolate chips (6 ounces)

1 cup dark (semi sweet)
chocolate chips (6 ounces)

1/2 cup butter

3/4 cup flour

1 1/2 cups sugar

1/2 cup
cocoa powder

1/4 teaspoon salt

1/4 teaspoon
baking soda

1/2 teaspoon
vanilla extract

2 eggs

TOOLS:

Oven
Baking pan (8x8 or larger)
Wax paper
Large bowl (x2)
Small bowl (x2)
Whisk
Rubber spatula
Measuring cups
Measuring spoons
Oven mitts

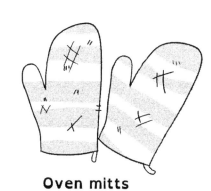

Oven mitts

Oven

Small bowl (x2)

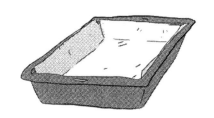

Baking pan (8x8 or larger)

Rubber spatula

Whisk

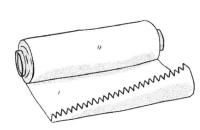

Wax paper

Large bowl (x2)

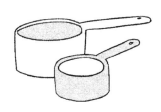

Measuring cups

Measuring spoons

INSTRUCTIONS

Step 1: Preheat oven 350 and line pan with wax paper. Melt butter in small bowl.

Step 2: Mix flour, cocoa powder, salt, and baking soda in a large bowl

Step 3: Mix sugar, melted butter, and vanilla extract in a separate bowl. Beat eggs into bowl one at a time.

Step 4: Slowly add dry bowl into wet bowl and mix thoroughly until even and smooth.

Step 5: Mix a little flour with the chocolate chips in a small bowl. Then mix into the batter evenly.

Step 6: Bake 25 minutes. Insert toothpick in middle of bread. If it comes out clean, it is done.

Step 7: Let cool in pan and behold the "basic deliciousness" of the Brownie.

MY RECIPE CHECKLIST

- ☐ Do I have all the ingredients
- ☐ Do I have all the tools
- ☐ Do I have permission
- ☐ Do I have a clock to watch the time
- ☐ Am I following all safety rules
- ☐ Have I followed all instructions
- ☐ Have I turned off all equipment
- ☐ Have I cleaned everything up
- ☐ Have I tasted it?

DRAW A PICTURE THE RECIPE,
YOUR RESULTS,
SOMETHING FUN ABOUT THE PROCESS,
OR SOMEONE EATING IT!

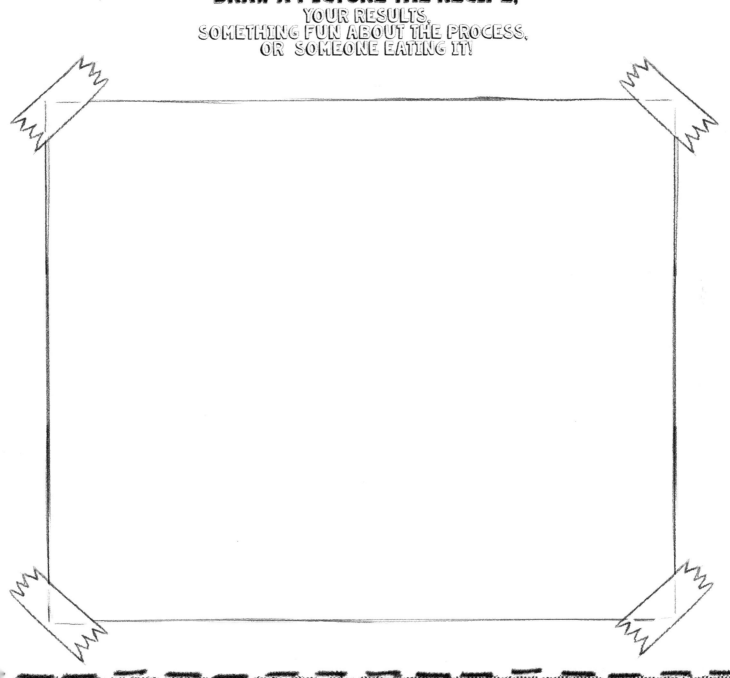

QUESTIONS & ANSWERS

HOW DID YOU LIKE THIS RECIPE?

HOW DID IT TASTE?

WHAT WAS DIFFICULT ABOUT MAKING IT?

WHAT DO YOU THINK COULD MAKE THIS RECIPE BETTER?

DID YOU LEARN ANYTHING NEW?

WHO DO YOU KNOW THAT WOULD LIKE THIS TREAT?

WORD SCRAMBLE

Use the letters shown to make the right "baking" words and phrases,
then fill them in the spaces below

AAULSPT   S _ _ _ _ _ _

OENV   O _ _ _

KHWSI   W _ _ _ _

OIEOKC   C _ _ _ _ _

THCCLOEAO   C _ _ _ _ _ _ _

TGSHGRTSEIE   S _ _ _   T _ _   E _ _

EEAHPRT   P _ _ _ _ _

KPBNGAIAN   B _ _ _ _ _   P _ _

HWHSTHSDSAIEE   W _ _ _   T _ _   D _ _ _ _ _

LLTCIEOO   L _ _ _   I _ _   C _ _

Below are pictures of the words and phrases to help you guess and for coloring:

CANDY BAR HEAVEN

INGREDIENTS:

Layer 1:
2 cups dark (semi sweet) chocolate chips (12 ounces)
1/3 cup peanut butter

Layer 2:
1/2 cup butter (1 stick)
3/4 cup granulated sugar
1/4 cup light brown sugar
1/4 cup evaporated milk
1/4 cup whipping cream
8 ounces marshmallows (1/2 standard bag)
1/3 cup peanut butter

Layer 3:
16 ounces caramel squares
1/4 cup heavy cream
1tablespoon butter

Layer 4:
2 cups dark chocolate
1/3 cup peanut butter

peanut butter

marshmallows

evaporated milk

whipping cream

caramel

granulated sugar

butter

chocolate chips

brown sugar

heavy cream

chocolate

TOOLS:

Stove
9x13 inch baking pan
Rubber Spatula
2 quart cooking pot
Big bowl
Measuring cups
Measuring spoons
Wax paper

Big bowl

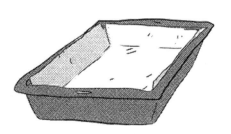

baking pan

Rubber Spatula

cooking pot

Stove

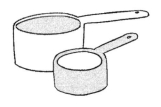

Measuring cups

Measuring spoons

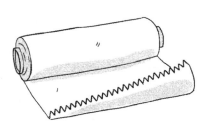

Wax paper

INSTRUCTIONS

Step 1: First Layer – Line baking pan with wax paper (long enough to drape sides)

Step 2: Mix chocolate chips and peanut butter in pan over low heat, stirring continually until smooth.

Step 3: Pour into baking pan and spread evenly with a spatula. Place in refrigerator for 30 minutes.

FOR 30 min.

Step 4:
Second layer – melt butter and whipping cream over medium heat in a pot. Add white sugar, brown sugar, and evaporated milk.

FOR 5 min.

Bring to boil and let boil for 5 minutes while stirring.

Step 5: Remove from stove; add marshmallows and peanut butter. Pour over chocolate layer and spread evenly with a spatula mixture. Place in refrigerator for 30 minutes.

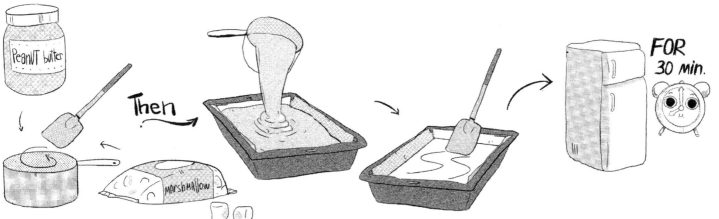

Then

FOR 30 min.

INSTRUCTIONS

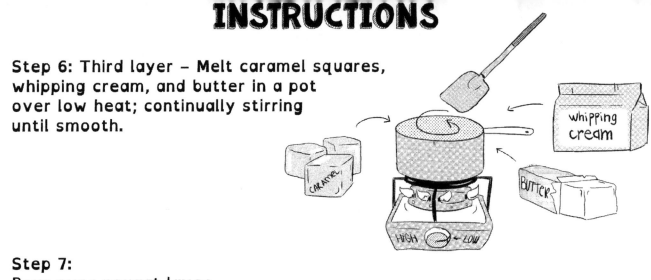

Step 6: Third layer – Melt caramel squares, whipping cream, and butter in a pot over low heat; continually stirring until smooth.

Step 7:
Pour over nougat layer and spread evenly with a spatula. Place back in refrigerator for 30 minutes.

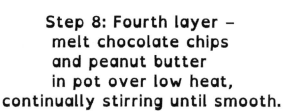

FOR 30 MIN.

Step 8: Fourth layer – melt chocolate chips and peanut butter in pot over low heat, continually stirring until smooth.

Step 9: Pour over the caramel layer and spread evenly with a spatula. Place back in refrigerator for 1 hour;

then cut this "Candy Bar Heaven" into squares.

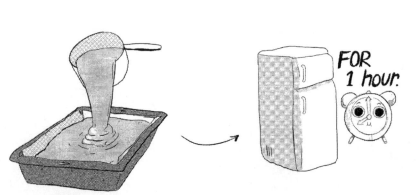

FOR 1 hour.

MY RECIPE CHECKLIST

- ☐ Do I have all the ingredients
- ☐ Do I have all the tools
- ☐ Do I have permission
- ☐ Do I have a clock to watch the time
- ☐ Am I following all safety rules
- ☐ Have I followed all instructions
- ☐ Have I turned off all equipment
- ☐ Have I cleaned everything up
- ☐ Have I tasted it?

DRAW A PICTURE THE RECIPE,
YOUR RESULTS,
SOMETHING FUN ABOUT THE PROCESS,
OR SOMEONE EATING IT!

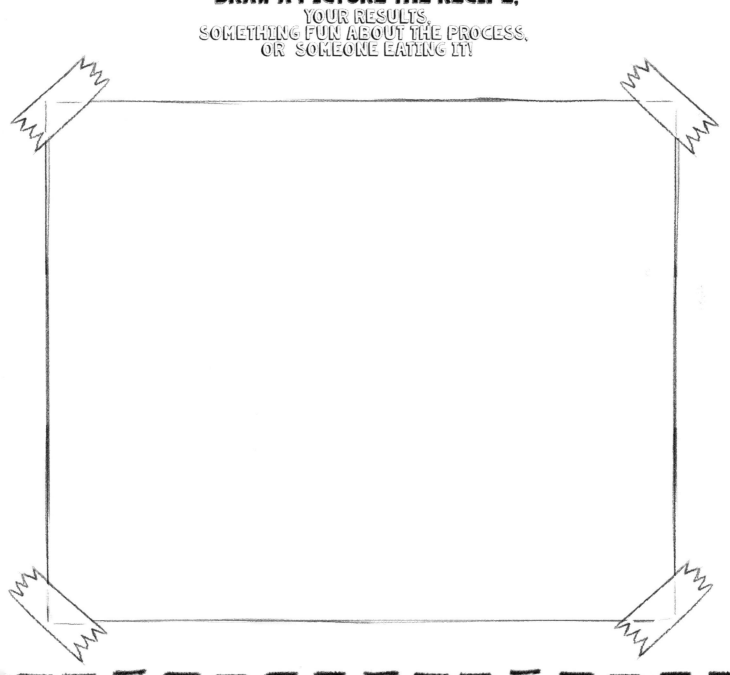

QUESTIONS & ANSWERS

HOW DID YOU LIKE THIS RECIPE?

- -

- -

HOW DID IT TASTE?

- -

- -

WHAT WAS DIFFICULT ABOUT MAKING IT?

- -

- -

- -

- -

WHAT DO YOU THINK COULD MAKE THIS RECIPE BETTER?

- -

- -

- -

- -

DID YOU LEARN ANYTHING NEW?

- -

- -

WHO DO YOU KNOW THAT WOULD LIKE THIS TREAT?

- -

- -

Now that you have finished 3 recipes it's time to further your education.
Watch a cooking show and try to duplicate a recipe,
read a book about baking, or maybe even a documentary about
how some treats are made.

In the bubbles below take notes and write 5 facts you learned

Write 5 new words you learned

1 -

2 -

3 -

4 -

5 -

Color the face above that shows how you feel about the video or book.

CHOCO-COFFEE CUPCAKES

INGREDIENTS:

2 cups flour
2 cups sugar
3/4 cup cocoa powder
1 teaspoon baking soda
1 teaspoon baking powder
1 teaspoon salt
2 large eggs
1/2 cup oil
1 cup milk
1 teaspoon vanilla extract
8 ounces black coffee cooled

flour

cocoa powder

sugar

oil

milk

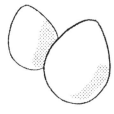

eggs

salt

baking powder

black coffee
(cooled)

baking soda

vanilla extract

TOOLS:

Oven
12-cup Muffin tin and liners (x2)
Whisk
Big spoon
Big bowl
Measuring cups
Measuring spoons
Oven mitts
Toothpick

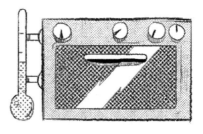

Oven

Muffin tin and liners

Whisk

Big spoon

Big bowl

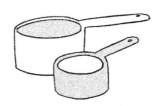

Measuring cups

Measuring spoons

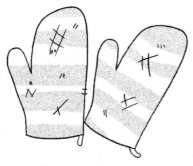

Oven mitts

Toothpick

INSTRUCTIONS

Step 1: Preheat oven to 350°F

and line two 12-cup muffin tins with liners.

Step 2: In a large bowl, whisk together
eggs, oil, vanilla, and black coffee (cooled).

Step 3: Add sugar, cocoa powder, salt,
baking soda and baking powder; and stir.

Step 4: Add flour and stir; then add milk and stir.

*If batter seems runny, don't worry;
this is normal and makes the cake moist.

INSTRUCTIONS

Step 5: Spoon batter into liners 3/4 full; filling 2 muffins tins.

Step 6: Bake for 20-25 minutes.

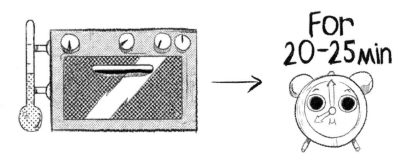

FOR 20-25min

Check with toothpick; if it comes out clean, it is done.

Toothpick

CLEAN

Step 7: after cooling, remove from tin and cover these "Choco-Coffee" treats with your favorite frosting or glaze.

MY RECIPE CHECKLIST

- ☐ Do I have all the ingredients
- ☐ Do I have all the tools
- ☐ Do I have permission
- ☐ Do I have a clock to watch the time
- ☐ Am I following all safety rules
- ☐ Have I followed all instructions
- ☐ Have I turned off all equipment
- ☐ Have I cleaned everything up
- ☐ Have I tasted it?

DRAW A PICTURE THE RECIPE,
YOUR RESULTS,
SOMETHING FUN ABOUT THE PROCESS,
OR SOMEONE EATING IT!

QUESTIONS & ANSWERS

HOW DID YOU LIKE THIS RECIPE?

....

....

HOW DID IT TASTE?

....

....

WHAT WAS DIFFICULT ABOUT MAKING IT?

....

....

....

....

WHAT DO YOU THINK COULD MAKE THIS RECIPE BETTER?

....

....

....

....

DID YOU LEARN ANYTHING NEW?

....

....

WHO DO YOU KNOW THAT WOULD LIKE THIS TREAT?

....

....

Mice need cheese, squirrels need nuts, and the boy needs a cookie.
follow the mazes below to help them find the way to what they need.

CHOCOLATE ÉCLAIRS

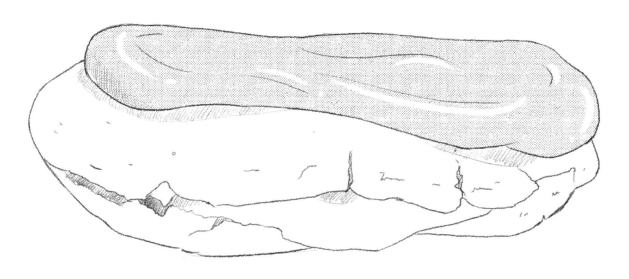

INGREDIENTS:

For the pastry:
1/2 cup butter (1 stick)
1 cup water
1/8 teaspoon salt
1 cup flour
4 eggs

For the filling:
2 egg whites
1/2 cup sugar
1/2 teaspoon lemon juice
1/2 teaspoon vanilla

For the glaze:
3/4 cup chocolate chips (4.5 ounces)
1/4 cup whipping cream
1 tablespoon honey

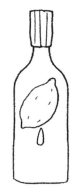
lemon juice

honey

butter

eggs

flour

whipping cream

sugar

vanilla

egg whites

salt

water

chocolate chips

TOOLS

Stove and oven
Cookie sheet
Wax paper
2 quart cooking pot
Double boiler
Rubber spatula
Large Bowl
Measuring cups
Measuring spoons
Piping bag
Oven mitts
Knife

Cookie sheet

oven

Knife

Piping bag

Big bowl

Rubber Spatula

Double boiler

cooking pot

Stove

Measuring cups

Measuring spoons

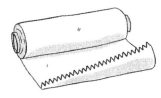
Wax paper

Oven mitts

INSTRUCTIONS

Step 1: Preheat oven to **425** and line cookie sheet with wax paper.

In pot: bring the butter, water, and salt to a boil over high heat.

Step **2**: Stir in flour all at once and continue to stir for **30** seconds.
Turn **off** the heat,
continuing to stir until in even and smooth.
Pour into large bowl and let cool 5 minutes.

Step **3**: Beat eggs in one at a time.
Pour into large pastry bag,
and cut a hole for a tip.

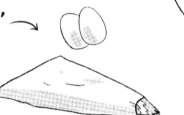

Step **4**: Pipe pastry onto lined cookie sheet.
Your pieces should be
3 inches long and 1 inch **wide**.

Step **5**: Bake **12** minutes.
Reduce to 350 and bake for 18 minutes
or
until slightly golden brown.
Cool before filling.

INSTRUCTIONS

Step 6: To make cream filling, add egg whites, sugar and lemon juice to double boiler and heat over simmering water. Whisking frequently, heat until egg whites become very frothy and sugar is dissolved.

Step 7: Add egg mixture and vanilla to **large** bowl and whisk vigorously **for at least 15 minutes** and it holds together.

Step 8: Transfer cream to pastry bag and cut hole for tip.

Cut Éclair in half and fill with cream.

Step 9: To make chocolate glaze, mix chocolate chips and whipping cream in pot on **low heat** ↳ until creamy.

Step 10: Dip the top of the éclair into chocolate.

Eat this

"Chocolate éclair" and pretend you are at a café in Paris!

MY RECIPE CHECKLIST

- [ ] Do I have all the ingredients
- [ ] Do I have all the tools
- [ ] Do I have permission
- [ ] Do I have a clock to watch the time
- [ ] Am I following all safety rules
- [ ] Have I followed all instructions
- [ ] Have I turned off all equipment
- [ ] Have I cleaned everything up
- [ ] Have I tasted it?

DRAW A PICTURE THE RECIPE,
YOUR RESULTS,
SOMETHING FUN ABOUT THE PROCESS,
OR SOMEONE EATING IT!

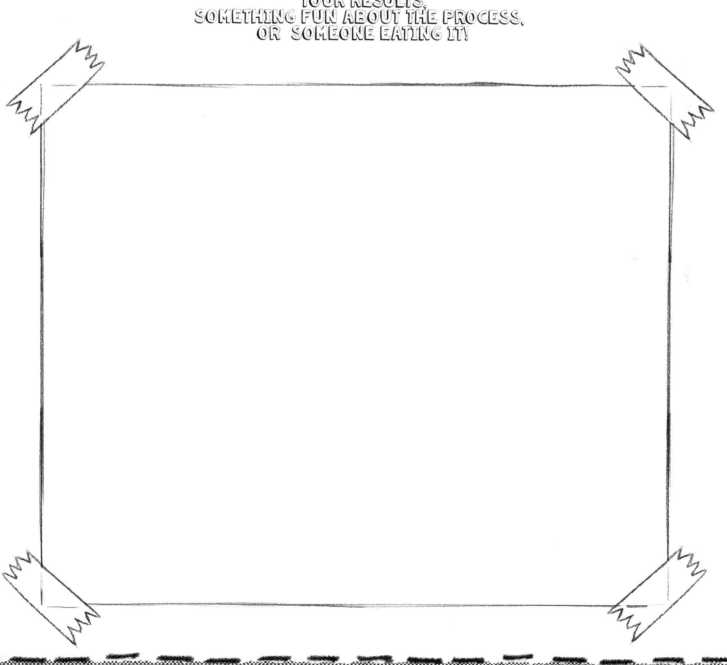

QUESTIONS & ANSWERS

HOW DID YOU LIKE THIS RECIPE?

HOW DID IT TASTE?

WHAT WAS DIFFICULT ABOUT MAKING IT?

WHAT DO YOU THINK COULD MAKE THIS RECIPE BETTER?

DID YOU LEARN ANYTHING NEW?

WHO DO YOU KNOW THAT WOULD LIKE THIS TREAT?

Let's make our own Recipe!

Now that you have worked on 5 recipes,
it's time to use your imagination and get creative.
You can take ideas from the recipes you have already worked on
or think up something completely new. Let's get started:

What do I want to make:

- -

- -

What ingredients do I need:

What tools do I need:

What are the instructions:

Let's give it a name:

- - - - - - - - - - - - - - - - - -

draw a picture of the recipe:

CHOCOLATE SANDIES

INGREDIENTS:

For the dough:
1 cup corn starch
2/3 cup flour
1/3 cup powder sugar
1/2 cup room temperature butter (1 stick)
* For something extra special,
add your favorite flavoring or extract to the mix.

For the chocolate:
1/2 cup dark (semi-sweet) chocolate chips
2/3 cup whipping cream

whipping cream

corn starch

powder sugar

flour

butter

chocolate chips

TOOLS:

Oven and Stove
2 quart cooking pot
Big bowl
Spatula
Measuring cup
Piping bag
Cooling rack
Cookie sheet
Wax paper
Oven mitts
Rolling pin

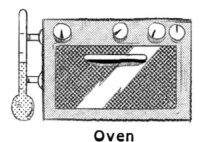
Oven

Stove

Measuring cup

Big bowl

Rolling pin

Spatula

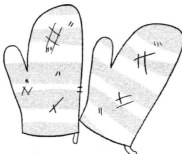
Oven mitts

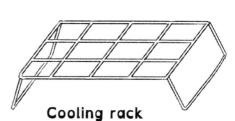
Cooling rack

Cookie sheet

Piping bag

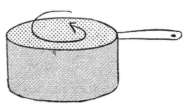
cooking pot

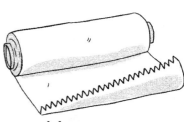
Wax paper

INSTRUCTIONS

Step 1: **preheat** oven to **350°F** and line cookie sheet with wax paper.

Step 2: **mix** room temperature butter with powder sugar until creamy.

Step 3: in a **separate** bowl,

sift **corn starch** and **flour**.

Step 4:

MiX butter mix

Step 5:

After dusting the counter with flour,

knead the dough into a **big** ball.

and then

Roll it out until 1inch thick

cut out cookie shapes.

INSTRUCTIONS

Step 6: **Transfer** cookies **one by one** onto cookie sheet.
Leave room of about **an inch** in between each cookie.

Step 7: put them in the oven for **10minutes** or until edges will become **light brown.**

Then take them out from the oven and put them on the cooling rack.

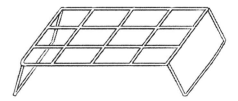

Step 8: pour Whipping cream into **pot.**
Let it warm over low heat, but do not let it boil.
Turn **off** stove, add chocolate, and blend until it has the consistency of a sauce.

Step 9: Let it cool to room temperature.

Spoon it into the piping bag.

Tie off the top of the bag.

Step 10: Cut the end of the piping bag (just a little) and decorate these "Sandies" with your imagination.

MY RECIPE CHECKLIST

- ☐ Do I have all the ingredients
- ☐ Do I have all the tools
- ☐ Do I have permission
- ☐ Do I have a clock to watch the time
- ☐ Am I following all safety rules
- ☐ Have I followed all instructions
- ☐ Have I turned off all equipment
- ☐ Have I cleaned everything up
- ☐ Have I tasted it?

DRAW A PICTURE THE RECIPE,
YOUR RESULTS,
SOMETHING FUN ABOUT THE PROCESS,
OR SOMEONE EATING IT!

QUESTIONS & ANSWERS

HOW DID YOU LIKE THIS RECIPE?

HOW DID IT TASTE?

WHAT WAS DIFFICULT ABOUT MAKING IT?

WHAT DO YOU THINK COULD MAKE THIS RECIPE BETTER?

DID YOU LEARN ANYTHING NEW?

WHO DO YOU KNOW THAT WOULD LIKE THIS TREAT?

There once was a king named Solomon. They say he was the wisest man to ever live.
He once told people to eat their bread with joy, because their work was accepted
(Ecclesiastes 9:7)
He knew that something yummy was always better
after we have done the things we are supposed to do.

Now draw a picture of a wise king enjoying a feast without a care in the world

Chores and homework are not always fun, but we enjoy our treats so much more
when we can relax
and not worry about everything we left undone.
Plus, parents love giving treats to
a child with a clean room more than to the child with a messy room.
What work do you need to complete before the next recipe?

- -

- -

- -

CLASSIC CHOCOLATE CHIP COOKIES

INGREDIENTS:

1/2 cup butter (1 stick)
1/2 cup sugar
1/4 cup light brown sugar
1 teaspoon vanilla extract
1 egg
1 3/4 cups flour
1/2 teaspoon baking soda
1/4 teaspoon salt
3/4 cup chocolate chips or chunks

light brown sugar

sugar

vanilla extract

flour

salt

baking soda

egg

butter

chocolate chips

TOOLS:

Oven
Cookie sheet
Wax paper
Large bowl
Rubber spatula
Whisk
Measuring cups
Measuring spoons
Oven mitts
Cooling rack

Oven

Measuring spoons

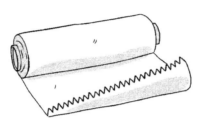
Wax paper

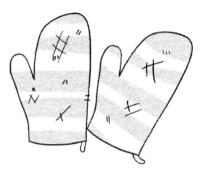
Oven mitts

Whisk

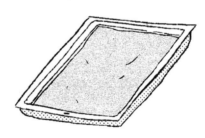
Cookie sheet

Rubber spatula

Large bowl

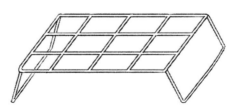
Cooling rack

Measuring cups

INSTRUCTIONS

Step 1: Preheat the oven to 350 and line cookie sheet with wax paper.

Step 2: melt butter until almost completely liquid.

Step 3: In Large bowl, beat butter **and** both sugars until creamy.

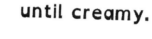

Mix in vanilla and egg until even and smooth.

Step 4: Add flour, baking soda, and salt; mix until crumbly.

Step 5: Add Chocolate chips and with your hands, press and mix it all together to form dough. It should be like one ball of dough that is not wet and not dry.

INSTRUCTIONS

Step 6: Roll dough into 12 large balls and place on a lined cookie sheet.

Step 7: Bake for 10 minutes or until the cookies look **puffy,** dry, and just barely golden.

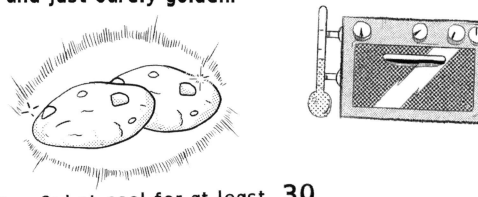

Step 8: Let cool for at least **30** minutes before eating these

"Classic Chocolate Chip Cookies".

MY RECIPE CHECKLIST

- ☐ Do I have all the ingredients
- ☐ Do I have all the tools
- ☐ Do I have permission
- ☐ Do I have a clock to watch the time
- ☐ Am I following all safety rules
- ☐ Have I followed all instructions
- ☐ Have I turned off all equipment
- ☐ Have I cleaned everything up
- ☐ Have I tasted it?

DRAW A PICTURE THE RECIPE,
YOUR RESULTS,
SOMETHING FUN ABOUT THE PROCESS,
OR SOMEONE EATING IT!

QUESTIONS & ANSWERS

HOW DID YOU LIKE THIS RECIPE?

- -

- -

HOW DID IT TASTE?

- -

- -

WHAT WAS DIFFICULT ABOUT MAKING IT?

- -

- -

- -

WHAT DO YOU THINK COULD MAKE THIS RECIPE BETTER?

- -

- -

- -

- -

DID YOU LEARN ANYTHING NEW?

- -

- -

WHO DO YOU KNOW THAT WOULD LIKE THIS TREAT?

- -

- -

Now that you have finished 7 recipes it's time to further your education.
Watch a cooking show and try to duplicate a recipe,
read a book about baking, or maybe even a documentary about
how some treats are made.

In the bubbles below take notes and write 5 facts you learned

Write 5 new words you learned

1 _

2 _

3 _

4 _

5 _

Color the face above that shows how you feel about the video or book.

CRISPY CARAMEL POPCORN

INGREDIENTS:

1 cup butter UNSALTED (2 sticks)
2 cups dark brown sugar
1/2 cups honey
1 tablespoon vanilla extract
1/2 teaspoon baking soda
6 quarts popcorn
(about 6 bags of microwave style)

butter

dark brown
sugar

honey

baking soda

vanilla extract

popcorn
(microwave style)

TOOLS:

Oven and stove
Large bowl
Cookie sheet (x2)
2 quart cooking pot
Wax paper
Measuring spoons
Rubber spatula

Stove

**2 quart
cooking pot**

Large bowl

Cookie sheet (x2)

Measuring spoons

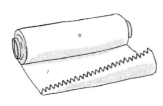

Wax paper

Rubber spatula

Oven

INSTRUCTIONS

Step 1: Preheat oven to 250 and line both cookie sheets with wax paper.

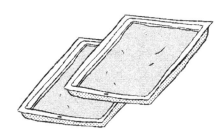

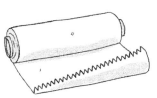

Place half the popcorn in a large bowl.

Step 2: In pot, mix honey and brown sugar on medium heat, stirring until melted. Raise heat and let boil **4 minutes.**

Step 3: Remove from heat and add vanilla and baking soda. It will bubble,

so stir quickly.

INSTRUCTIONS

Step 4: Pour half of the caramel **over** popcorn in bowl,

stirring well to coat.

Add the other half the popcorn to bowl.
Pour remaining caramel over popcorn, *stirring again.*

Step 5: Evenly spread popcorn on the two pans.
Bake for one hour, stirring every 15 minutes to spread caramel.

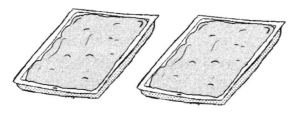

Step 6: As it cools continue to stir
and break up the larger pieces into small ones.

Store in an airtight container.
Share this "Crispy Caramel Popcorn" with those you love.

MY RECIPE CHECKLIST

- ☐ Do I have all the ingredients
- ☐ Do I have all the tools
- ☐ Do I have permission
- ☐ Do I have a clock to watch the time
- ☐ Am I following all safety rules
- ☐ Have I followed all instructions
- ☐ Have I turned off all equipment
- ☐ Have I cleaned everything up
- ☐ Have I tasted it?

DRAW A PICTURE THE RECIPE,
YOUR RESULTS,
SOMETHING FUN ABOUT THE PROCESS,
OR SOMEONE EATING IT!

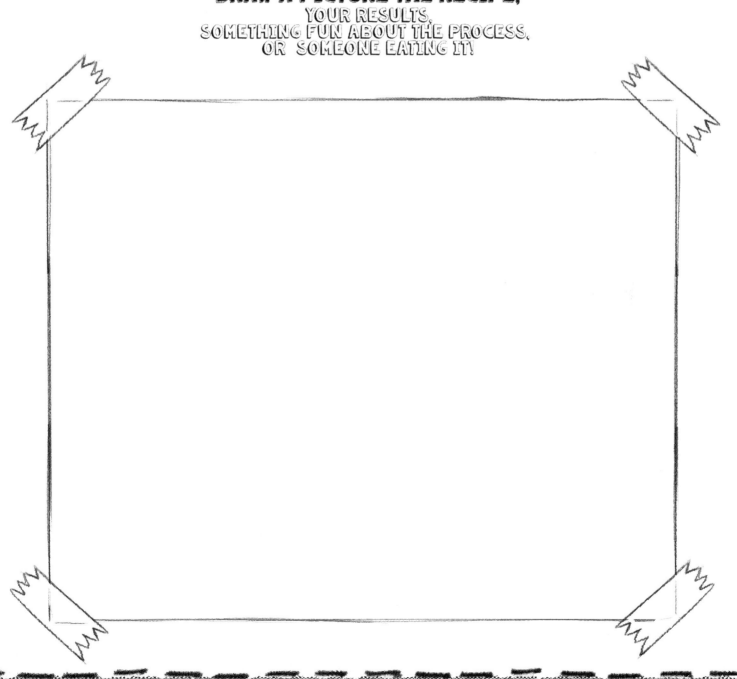

QUESTIONS & ANSWERS

HOW DID YOU LIKE THIS RECIPE?

- -

- -

HOW DID IT TASTE?

- -

- -

WHAT WAS DIFFICULT ABOUT MAKING IT?

- -

- -

- -

WHAT DO YOU THINK COULD MAKE THIS RECIPE BETTER?

- -

- -

- -

- -

DID YOU LEARN ANYTHING NEW?

- -

- -

WHO DO YOU KNOW THAT WOULD LIKE THIS TREAT?

- -

- -

The baker has to get to his cake. follow this maze to get him there. Don't get lost at the cookie or pie

CRISPY GOODNESS BARS

INGREDIENTS:

Layer 1
12 ounces cereal (balls, loops, flakes, or shapes)
8 ounces marshmallow (1/2 standard bag)
3 tablespoons butter
1 teaspoon vanilla extract

Layer 2
16 ounces caramel squares
1/2 cup butter (1 stick)
1/4 cup whipping cream
1 teaspoon vanilla extract

Layer 3
16 ounces dark (semi-sweet) chocolate chips
1/2 cup heavy cream
1/2 cup butter (1 stick)
1 teaspoon vanilla extract

cereal

butter

vanilla

heavy cream

whipping cream

caramel
squares

TOOLS:

Stove
8 x 13 inch baking pan
Wax paper
2 quart cooking pot
Whisk
Rubber spatula
Big bowl
Measuring cups
Measuring spoons
Refrigerator
Knife
Little bowl with water

Stove

8 x 13 inch
baking pan

Rubber spatula

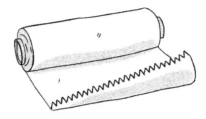

Wax paper

Little bowl with water

Big bowl

Knife

Measuring spoons

Measuring cups

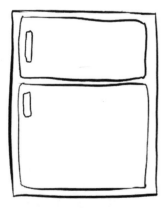

Refrigerator

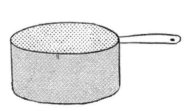

2 quart
cooking pot

Whisk

INSTRUCTIONS

Step 1: first layer – put cereal in a bowl and wax paper

in the baking pan.

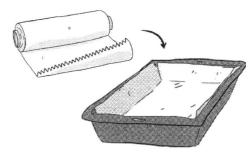

Step 2: Put marshmallows and butter in a pot; place on stove over low heat. Mix until melted and creamy. Remove from stove, add vanilla, and mix well.

 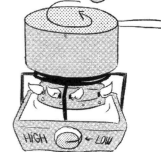

Step 3: Immediately mix with cereal and put in pan. With wet hands, even out the mix in the pan (marshmallow will not stick to wet hands). Place in refrigerator to cool.

Step 4: Second layer – heat butter and whipping cream in a pot over low heat. Slowly add caramel squares and stir until melted. Remove from stove, add vanilla, and mix well.

Step 5: Pour caramel over cereal layer and spread evenly with a spatula. Place back in refrigerator for 20-30 minutes.

INSTRUCTIONS

Step 6: Third layer – heat butter and whipping cream in a pot over low heat.
Add chocolate chips and stir until melted.
Remove from stove, add vanilla, and mix well.

Step 7: Pour chocolate over caramel layer and spread evenly with a spatula.
Place back in refrigerator for 1hour.

Step 8: Take this "Crispy Goodness" out of the refrigerator, very carefully flip it over

...very carefully

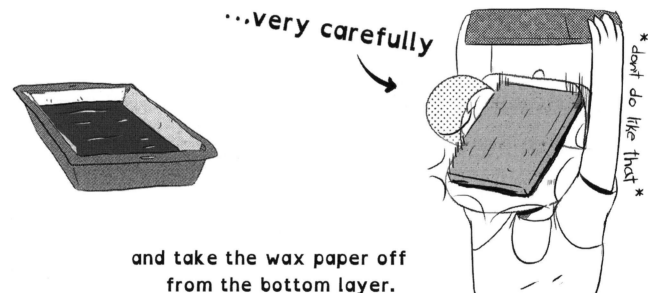

* don't do like that *

and take the wax paper off
from the bottom layer.

Flip it again (chocolate on the top)
cut into candy-bar sized pieces with a knife.

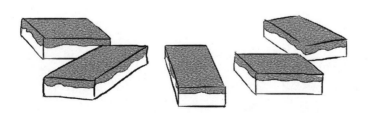

MY RECIPE CHECKLIST

- ☐ Do I have all the ingredients
- ☐ Do I have all the tools
- ☐ Do I have permission
- ☐ Do I have a clock to watch the time
- ☐ Am I following all safety rules
- ☐ Have I followed all instructions
- ☐ Have I turned off all equipment
- ☐ Have I cleaned everything up
- ☐ Have I tasted it?

DRAW A PICTURE THE RECIPE,
YOUR RESULTS,
SOMETHING FUN ABOUT THE PROCESS,
OR SOMEONE EATING IT!

QUESTIONS & ANSWERS

HOW DID YOU LIKE THIS RECIPE?

HOW DID IT TASTE?

WHAT WAS DIFFICULT ABOUT MAKING IT?

WHAT DO YOU THINK COULD MAKE THIS RECIPE BETTER?

DID YOU LEARN ANYTHING NEW?

WHO DO YOU KNOW THAT WOULD LIKE THIS TREAT?

What is your favorite yummy treat?

- -

- -

Go to a library or use the internet (with your parent's permission)
to find out as much information as you can about this treat.
Write a report about what you learned below. Make sure to include: where it was
invented, who created it,and any other interesting facts.

When you are done with that draw a picture of the treat.

- -

- -

- -

- -

- -

- -

- -

- -

- -

- -

GINGERBREAD GUYS AND GALS

INGREDIENTS:

For Cookie:
5 cups all flour
1 1/2 teaspoon baking soda
1/2 teaspoon salt
1 teaspoon ground ginger
 1 tablespoon cinnamon
1/2 teaspoon cloves
1/2 cup butter
1cup molasses
1 egg
1/2 cup sugar

For Icing:
1 egg white
2 cups powdered sugar
1/4 cup lemon juice

flour

lemon juice

salt

baking soda

powdered sugar

sugar

egg white

egg

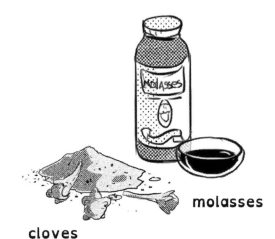

molasses

cloves

butter

ground ginger

cinnamon

TOOLS:

Oven
Cookie sheet
Wax paper
Large bowl (x2)
Rubber spatula
Measuring cup
Measuring spoon
Whisk
Rolling pin
Piping bag
Cooling rack
Oven mitts
Cookie cutters
(gingerbread man)

Oven

Cookie sheet

Cookie cutters
(gingerbread man)

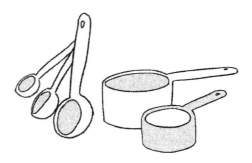

Large bowl

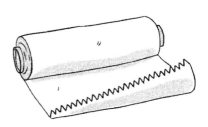

Wax paper

Rolling pin

Rubber spatula

Measuring spoon

Measuring cup

Whisk

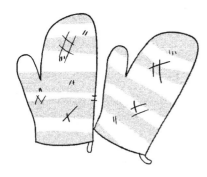

Oven mitts

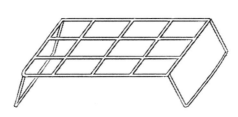

Cooling rack

Piping bag

INSTRUCTIONS

Step 1: Preheat oven to 350
and line cookie sheet with wax paper.

 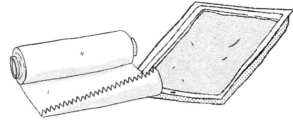

Step 2: Cream butter and sugar in bowl until it is light and fluffy.

Mix in egg and molasses until even and smooth.

 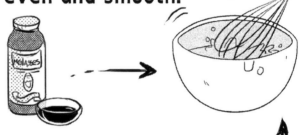

Step 3: In separate bowl mix flour, baking soda,
salt and spices. Slowly add dry bowl into wet bowl.
Mix thoroughly.

Step 4: Place in refrigerator for 4 hours.
Then roll dough out to 1/2 inch thickness.
Cut with cookie cutters.

INSTRUCTIONS

Step 5: Put cookies on lined cookie sheet.
Bake for up to 12 minutes or until edges are light brown.

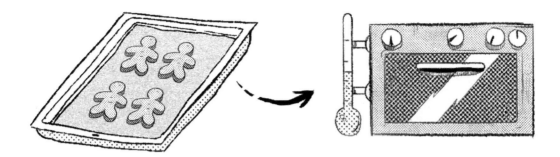

Step 6: Place cookies on cooling rack.

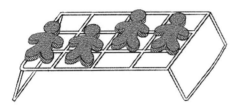

Step 7: To make the icing: whisk the egg white, powdered sugar, and lemon juice until smooth.

Step 8: Fill piping bag with the icing and decorate these "gingerbread guys and gals".

It's also fun using sprinkles, candies, and other toppings.

MY RECIPE CHECKLIST

- ☐ Do I have all the ingredients
- ☐ Do I have all the tools
- ☐ Do I have permission
- ☐ Do I have a clock to watch the time
- ☐ Am I following all safety rules
- ☐ Have I followed all instructions
- ☐ Have I turned off all equipment
- ☐ Have I cleaned everything up
- ☐ Have I tasted it?

DRAW A PICTURE THE RECIPE,
YOUR RESULTS,
SOMETHING FUN ABOUT THE PROCESS,
OR SOMEONE EATING IT!

QUESTIONS & ANSWERS

HOW DID YOU LIKE THIS RECIPE?

HOW DID IT TASTE?

WHAT WAS DIFFICULT ABOUT MAKING IT?

WHAT DO YOU THINK COULD MAKE THIS RECIPE BETTER?

DID YOU LEARN ANYTHING NEW?

WHO DO YOU KNOW THAT WOULD LIKE THIS TREAT?

Let's make our own Recipe!

Now that you have worked on 10 recipes,
it's time to use your imagination and get creative.
You can take ideas from the recipes you have already worked on
or think up something completely new. Let's get started:

What do I want to make:

- -

- -

What ingredients do I need:

-      -

-      -

-      -

-      -

-      -

-      -

What tools do I need:

-      -

-      -

-      -

-      -

-      -

-      -

What are the instructions:

- -

- -

- -

- -

- -

Let's give it a name:

- -

draw a picture of the recipe:

GUILT-FREE CHOCOLATE BITES

INGREDIENTS:

This recipe lets you mix and match to fit your taste!

 8 ounces dark chocolate
(The higher percentage of cacao the better)
Assorted dried fruits:
Raisins, dried cranberries, chopped dried apricots, dates, figs
Assorted chopped nuts:
 Almonds, walnuts, pistachio, hazelnuts
Other ingredients:
Seeds, cookies crumbs, cherries, coconut shavings, etc.

chocolate

cherries,

Seeds,

cookies crumbs,

coconut shavings

Almonds,

walnuts,

pistachio,

hazelnuts

TOOLS:

Microwave
Glass measuring cup
Spoon
Cutting board
Knife
wax paper
Cookie sheet

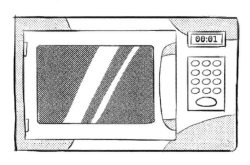

Microwave

Spoon

Knife

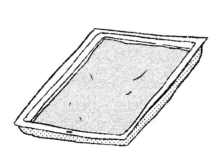

Cookie sheet

Glass
measuring cup

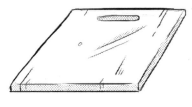

Cutting board

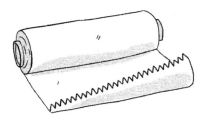

wax paper

INSTRUCTIONS

Step 1: line a cookie sheet with wax paper.

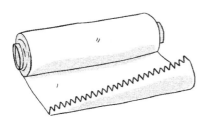 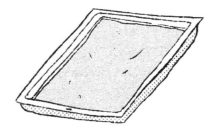

Step 2: Chop chocolate into small pieces
and microwave for 60 seconds in glass measuring cup; then stir.
Microwave for 30 seconds more and stir again to completely melt chocolate.
Repeat if there are still chunks.

 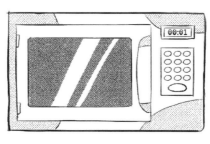 

Step 3: Use a spoon to make small rounds of chocolate on the wax paper.
Sprinkle each chocolate round with your nuts, fruits,
 and other add-ins while chocolate is still hot. A 2 inch diameter is a good size.

Step 4: refrigerate for 60 minutes to cool.
 Feel free to eat these healthy chocolate "guilt-free"!

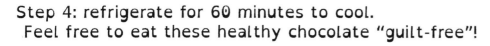

MY RECIPE CHECKLIST

- ☐ Do I have all the ingredients
- ☐ Do I have all the tools
- ☐ Do I have permission
- ☐ Do I have a clock to watch the time
- ☐ Am I following all safety rules
- ☐ Have I followed all instructions
- ☐ Have I turned off all equipment
- ☐ Have I cleaned everything up
- ☐ Have I tasted it?

DRAW A PICTURE THE RECIPE,
YOUR RESULTS,
SOMETHING FUN ABOUT THE PROCESS,
OR SOMEONE EATING IT!

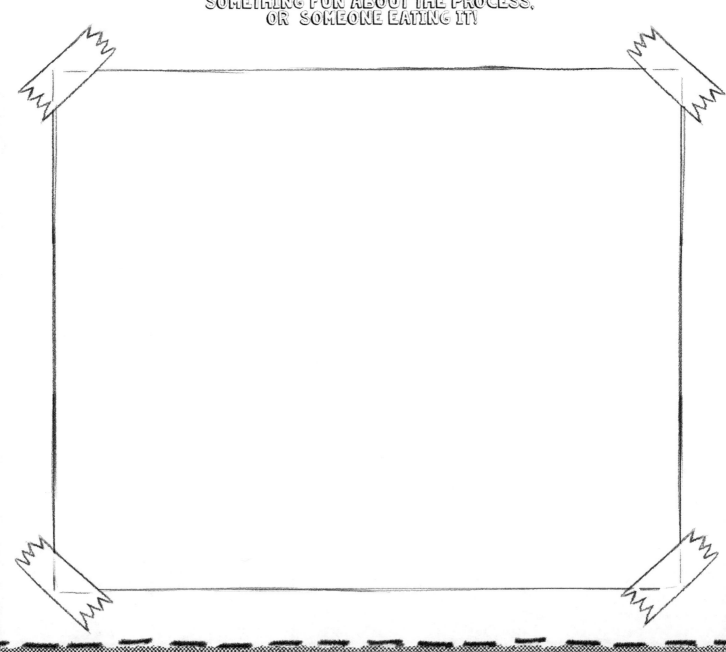

QUESTIONS & ANSWERS

HOW DID YOU LIKE THIS RECIPE?

HOW DID IT TASTE?

WHAT WAS DIFFICULT ABOUT MAKING IT?

WHAT DO YOU THINK COULD MAKE THIS RECIPE BETTER?

DID YOU LEARN ANYTHING NEW?

WHO DO YOU KNOW THAT WOULD LIKE THIS TREAT?

At this point you have created a lot of yummy treats.
It is a good time to remind you that cakes
and cookies are so good,but only in reasonable amounts.Homework is good for you
too,but too much can make your head hurt.
Too many sweets can give you tummy troubles.
Every boy and girl should also eat lots of vegetables and fruits every day.
They are so good for you, filled with all sorts of good stuff to
make you strong and healthy.
A songwriter once said that we should fill our hungry soul with what is good
(Psalm 107:9).

write the names of these fruits and veggies before coloring them in.

Are there any other things you can think of where too much can be unhealthy?

- -

- -

What are some alternatives to those things?

- -

- -

HAVAIIAN COOKIES

INGREDIENTS:

2 bananas (the browner the better)
2 1/2 cups oats
2 eggs
1 cup sugar
2 teaspoons baking soda
2 tablespoons molasses
3/4 cup sweetened coconut flakes
1 cup milk
1/2 cup raisins
1/2 cup dried cranberries
1/2 cup dark (semi sweet) chocolate chips (3 ounces)

dried cranberries

oats

sugar

soda

bananas

milk

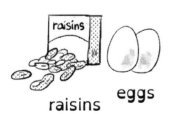

raisins   eggs

sweetened coconut

flakes

molasses

chocolate chips

TOOLS:

Oven
Cookie sheet
Large Bowl
Wax paper
Rubber spatula
Fork
Measuring cups
Measuring spoons
Oven mitts
Cooling rack

Oven

Cookie sheet

Large Bowl   Rubber spatula

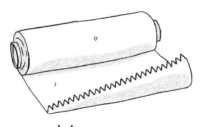
Wax paper

Fork

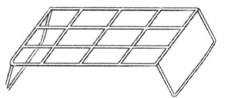
Cooling rack

Measuring spoons   Measuring cups

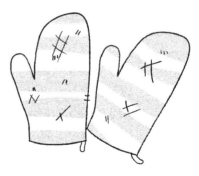
Oven mitts

INSTRUCTIONS

Step 1: Preheat oven to 350 and line cookie sheet with wax paper.

 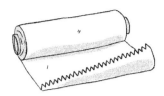

Step 2: In a large bowl, mash bananas with fork. Add eggs, sugar, baking soda, and molasses. Stir until well blended.

Step 3: Pour in oats, coconut flakes and milk; mixing until evenly distributed.

Step 4: Pour in raisins, cranberries, and chocolate; mixing until evenly distributed. Let sit for 40 minutes

Step 5: Drop spoonfuls onto lined cookie sheet (leave a space of 2 inches around).

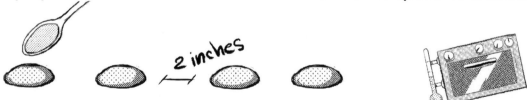

Step 6: Bake 10 minutes or until edges are golden-brown.

Step 7: Let cool 5 minutes before transferring to cooling rack. Host a luau and enjoy these "Hawaiian cookies"!

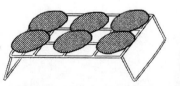

MY RECIPE CHECKLIST

- ☐ Do I have all the ingredients
- ☐ Do I have all the tools
- ☐ Do I have permission
- ☐ Do I have a clock to watch the time
- ☐ Am I following all safety rules
- ☐ Have I followed all instructions
- ☐ Have I turned off all equipment
- ☐ Have I cleaned everything up
- ☐ Have I tasted it?

DRAW A PICTURE THE RECIPE,
YOUR RESULTS,
SOMETHING FUN ABOUT THE PROCESS,
OR SOMEONE EATING IT!

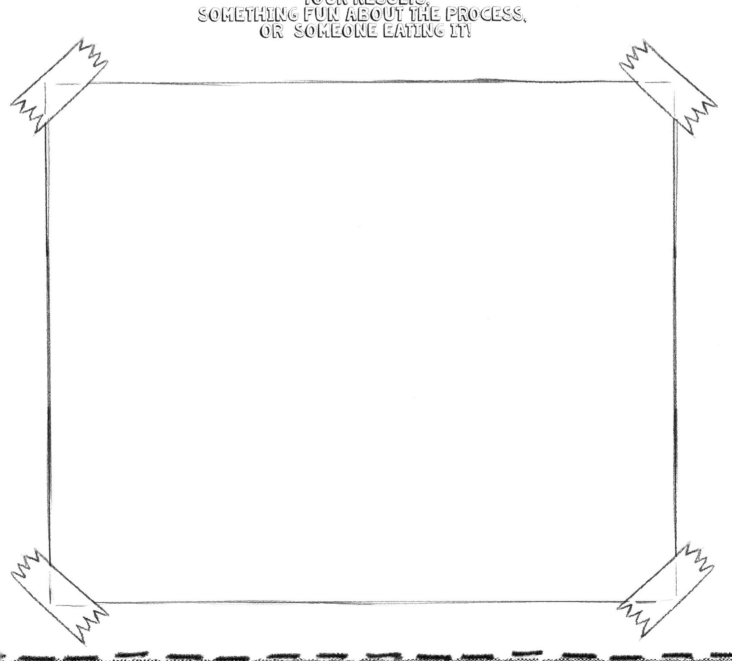

QUESTIONS & ANSWERS

HOW DID YOU LIKE THIS RECIPE?

HOW DID IT TASTE?

WHAT WAS DIFFICULT ABOUT MAKING IT?

WHAT DO YOU THINK COULD MAKE THIS RECIPE BETTER?

DID YOU LEARN ANYTHING NEW?

WHO DO YOU KNOW THAT WOULD LIKE THIS TREAT?

Now that you have finished 12 recipes it's time to further your education.
Watch a cooking show and try to duplicate a recipe,
read a book about baking, or maybe even a documentary about
how some treats are made.

In the bubbles below take notes and write 5 facts you learned

Write 5 new words you learned

1 _

2 _

3 _

4 _

5 _

Color the face above that shows how you feel about the video or book.

HOME-STYLE PEANUT BUTTER CHEESECAKE

INGREDIENTS:

For the Crust:
1 1/2 cups graham cracker crumbs (1 package)
1/3 cup sugar
1/3 cup butter

For the Filling:
24 ounces softened cream cheese (3 packs)
1 1/2 cups sugar
4 eggs, separated
1 Tablespoon lemon juice
1 teaspoon vanilla extract

For the Peanut butter layer:
1 cup creamy peanut butter
1/2 cup whipping cream

Chocolate top:
3/4 cup dark (semi sweet) chocolate chips (4.5 ounces)
1/2 cup whipping cream

eggs

vanilla

whipping
cream

softened cream
cheese

sugar

butter

graham cracker
crumbs

peanut butter

lemon juice

chocolate chips

TOOLS:

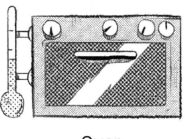
Oven

Oven and stove
Pie tin or cake pan
2 quart cooking pot
Large bowl (x2)
Rubber spatula
Measuring cups
Measuring spoons
Oven mitts

Large bowl

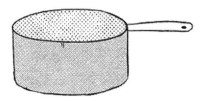
cooking pot

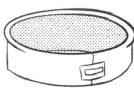
cake pan

Rubber spatula

stove

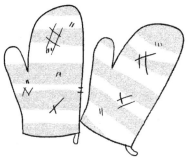
Oven mitts

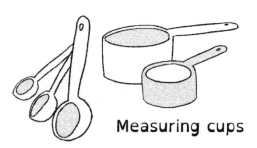
Measuring cups

Measuring spoons

INSTRUCTIONS

Step 1: Preheat oven to 325
and line pie tin or cake pan with wax paper to prepare for crust.

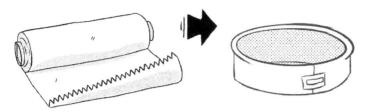

Step 2: In large bowl, melt butter.
Add "Crust" ingredients and mix.
Pour into tin and press against sides and bottom.

Step 3: For the filling: In large bowl thoroughly mix cream cheese,
sugar, 4 egg yolks, lemon juice and vanilla.

Step 4: In a separate bowl, beat 4 egg whites until

stiff and creamy.

Step 5: Fold egg whites into cream cheese mixture.

 Pour into crust.

INSTRUCTIONS

Step 6: Bake for 35 minutes.
Turn off oven and leave inside with door closed for 1 hour.

Step 7: Stir peanut butter and whipping cream in pot on medium heat until smooth.
Pour over cheesecake.

Step 8: let sit for 30 minutes,
allowing peanut butter layer to firm.

Step 8: Stir Chocolate chips and whipping cream in pot on medium heat until smooth
Pour over cheesecake

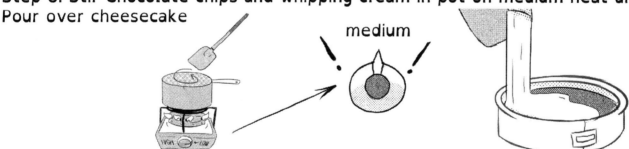

Step 9: Put in freezer for at least 2 hours before serving.
Allow to cheesecake thaw. Chill out with this Peanut Butter cheesecake.
This is what home-style is all about!

MY RECIPE CHECKLIST

- ☐ Do I have all the ingredients
- ☐ Do I have all the tools
- ☐ Do I have permission
- ☐ Do I have a clock to watch the time
- ☐ Am I following all safety rules
- ☐ Have I followed all instructions
- ☐ Have I turned off all equipment
- ☐ Have I cleaned everything up
- ☐ Have I tasted it?

DRAW A PICTURE THE RECIPE,
YOUR RESULTS,
SOMETHING FUN ABOUT THE PROCESS,
OR SOMEONE EATING IT!

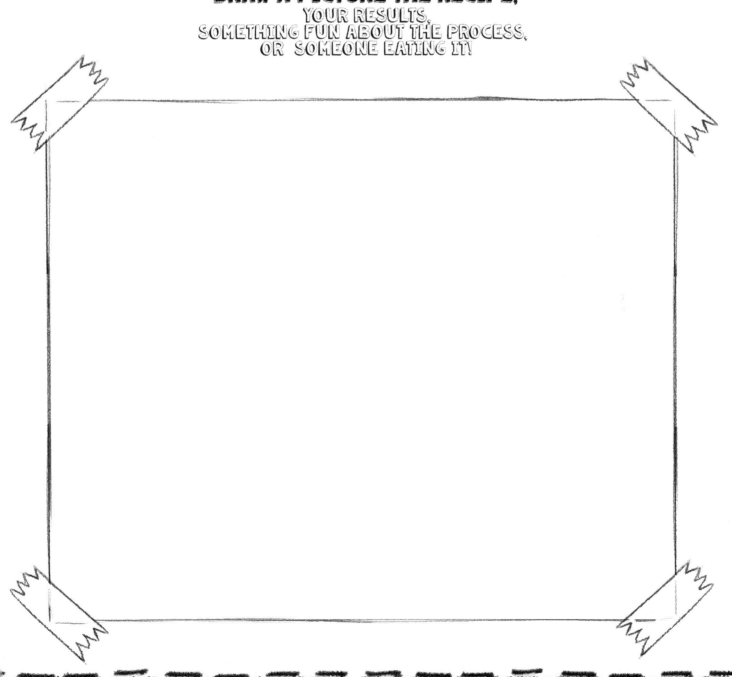

QUESTIONS & ANSWERS

HOW DID YOU LIKE THIS RECIPE?

- -

- -

HOW DID IT TASTE?

- -

- -

WHAT WAS DIFFICULT ABOUT MAKING IT?

- -

- -

- -

- -

WHAT DO YOU THINK COULD MAKE THIS RECIPE BETTER?

- -

- -

- -

- -

DID YOU LEARN ANYTHING NEW?

- -

WHO DO YOU KNOW THAT WOULD LIKE THIS TREAT?

- -

We already know that we can't have sweet treats all the time.
We know that we need to fill our body with good things like fruits and vegetables.
But if we want to stay healthy, we also need to stay active.
There are many ways of doing this. Some people play sports or lift weights,
others like to dance and play games, and some like to do hard work
like cleaning or building.

What do you do to stay active?

- -

- -

Try something new today to stay and then write about it:

- -

- -

- -

Do you like working out alone or with a friend, why?

- -

- -

Draw a picture of your favorite way to stay fit

HONEYCAKE

INGREDIENTS:

1 cup honey
1 cup strong black tea
2/3 cup melted butter
3 1/3 cups flour
1 teaspoon baking soda
½ cup chopped dried apricots
½ cup chopped nuts (any variety)

dried apricots

honey

butter

baking soda

strong
black tea

chopped nuts

TOOLS:

Oven
Baking pan (8x8 or larger)
Wax paper
2 quart cooking pot
Large bowl
Small bowl
Rubber spatula
Measuring cups
Measuring spoons
Oven mitts

Oven

Large bowl

Small bowl

Rubber spatula

Wax paper

Measuring spoons

Measuring cups

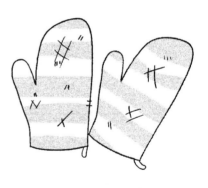

Oven mitts

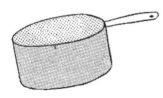

2 quart cooking pot

Baking pan

INSTRUCTIONS

Step 1: Preheat oven 350 and line pan with wax paper. Melt butter in small bowl.

Step 2: Pour honey and hot tea

in a large bowl pour,

and let dissolve.

Step 3: Mix in melted butter and flour thoroughly until smooth.

Step 4: Stir in dried apricots until evenly distributed.
Pour into line baking pan and sprinkle with nuts.

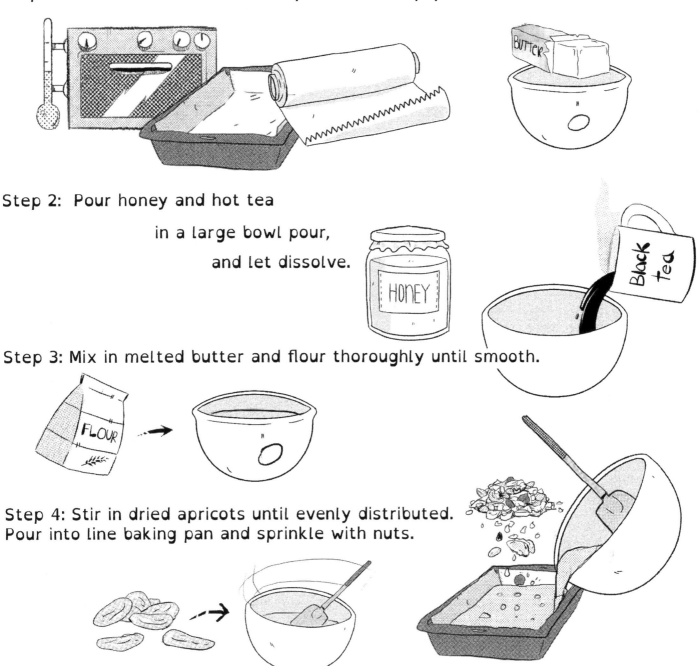

Step 5: Bake 40 minutes. Insert toothpick in middle of bread. If it comes out clean, it is done.

Step 6: Let cool in pan and let your life be a little sweeter with this "Honeycake".

MY RECIPE CHECKLIST

- ☐ Do I have all the ingredients
- ☐ Do I have all the tools
- ☐ Do I have permission
- ☐ Do I have a clock to watch the time
- ☐ Am I following all safety rules
- ☐ Have I followed all instructions
- ☐ Have I turned off all equipment
- ☐ Have I cleaned everything up
- ☐ Have I tasted it?

DRAW A PICTURE THE RECIPE,
YOUR RESULTS,
SOMETHING FUN ABOUT THE PROCESS,
OR SOMEONE EATING IT!

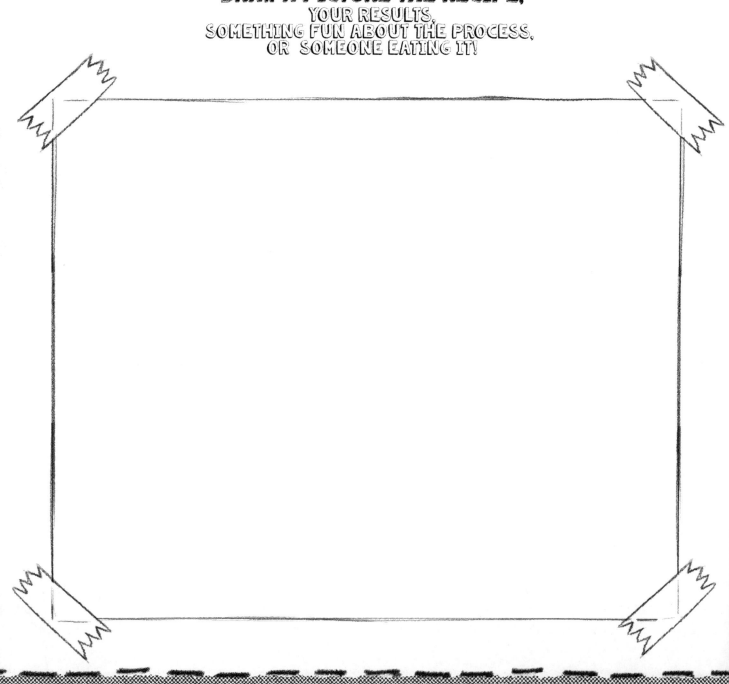

QUESTIONS & ANSWERS

HOW DID YOU LIKE THIS RECIPE?

HOW DID IT TASTE?

WHAT WAS DIFFICULT ABOUT MAKING IT?

WHAT DO YOU THINK COULD MAKE THIS RECIPE BETTER?

DID YOU LEARN ANYTHING NEW?

WHO DO YOU KNOW THAT WOULD LIKE THIS TREAT?

REASSEMBLE THIS PICTURE

In the empty boxes below mark the letter of the piece of the broken picture that fits to make the picture whole again.

JAMMIE CAKE

INGREDIENTS:

For Cake:
2 eggs
1/2 cup sugar
3 1/4 cups flour
1/4 teaspoon vanilla
1 1/2 teaspoon baking powder
1 pinch of salt
1 cup frozen butter (2 sticks)

For filling:
2/3 cup fruit preserves or jam (any flavor)
1 cup flour

flour

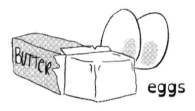

butter   eggs

jam

vanilla   baking powder

salt   sugar

TOOLS:

Oven
Baking pan (8x8 or larger)
Wax paper
Large bowls (x2)
Small bowl
Whisk
Grater
Large plate
Rubber spatula
Measuring cups
Measuring spoons
Oven mitts

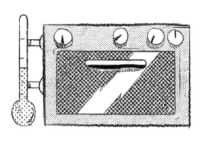

Oven

Large bowls

Small bowl

Baking pan

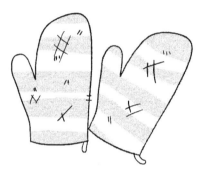

Oven mitts

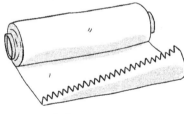

Wax paper

Whisk

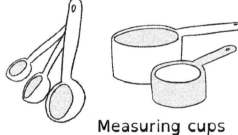

Measuring cups

Measuring spoons

Rubber spatula

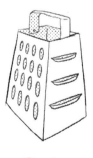

Grater

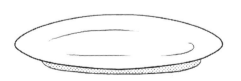

Large plate

INSTRUCTIONS

Step 1: Preheat oven to 350 and line baking pan with wax paper.

Step 2: In large bowl mix 3 cups flour, baking powder, vanilla, and salt thoroughly and evenly.

Step 3: Grate butter and add to bowl. Mix together with hands.

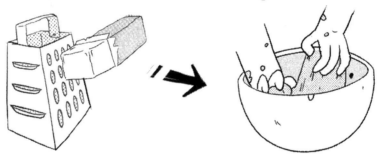

Step 4: In a separate bowl thoroughly mix eggs and sugar until smooth. Pour into flour bowl and mix until even.

Step 5: Knead the dough for while, then add the remaining flour and knead until ready.

INSTRUCTIONS

Step 6: Separate the dough into 2 parts. Leave one part in bowl and place in refrigerator.
Separate the remaining dough into 5 balls,
place on a large plate in the freezer for 40 minutes.

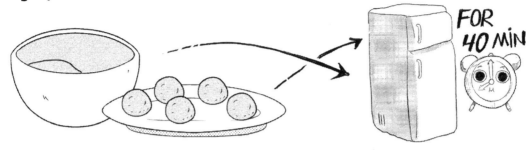

Step 7: After 40 minutes take dough from refrigerator and spread across lined baking dish.

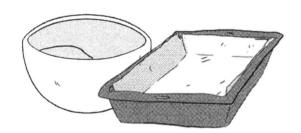
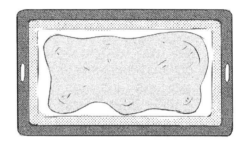

Step 8: mix jam with flour and spread evenly across the cake.

Step 9: Take dough from freezer and grate them over the top of the cake evenly

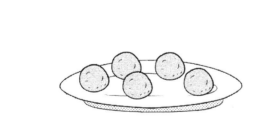

Step 10: Bake for 35 minutes until pale golden-brown. Let cool.

Put on pajamas and have this "Jammie Cake".

MY RECIPE CHECKLIST

- [x] Do I have all the ingredients
- [x] Do I have all the tools
- [x] Do I have permission
- [x] Do I have a clock to watch the time
- [x] Am I following all safety rules
- [x] Have I followed all instructions
- [x] Have I turned off all equipment
- [x] Have I cleaned everything up
- [ ] Have I tasted it?

DRAW A PICTURE THE RECIPE,
YOUR RESULTS,
SOMETHING FUN ABOUT THE PROCESS,
OR SOMEONE EATING IT!

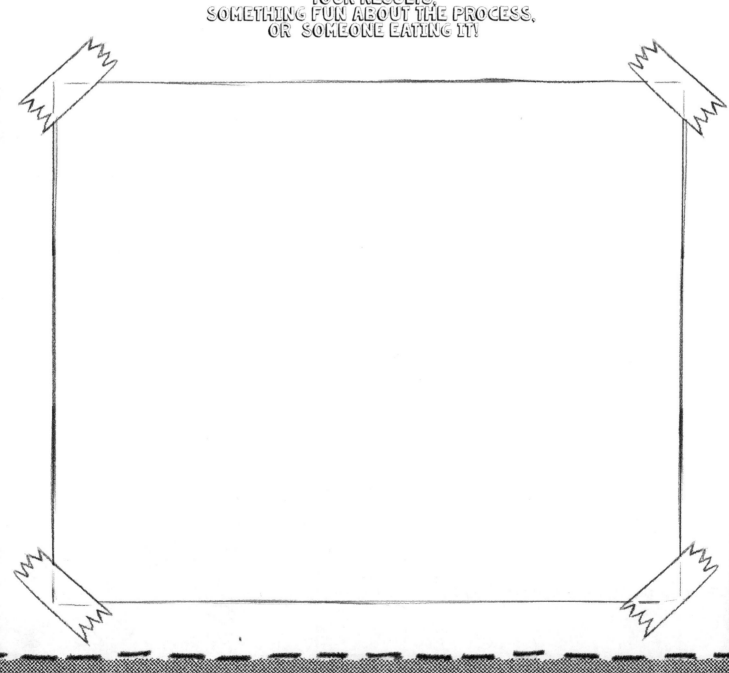

QUESTIONS & ANSWERS

HOW DID YOU LIKE THIS RECIPE?

HOW DID IT TASTE?

Good

WHAT WAS DIFFICULT ABOUT MAKING IT?

Stirring

WHAT DO YOU THINK COULD MAKE THIS RECIPE BETTER?

Add milk so It's not so dry

DID YOU LEARN ANYTHING NEW?

no

WHO DO YOU KNOW THAT WOULD LIKE THIS TREAT?

Daddy

Let's make our own Recipe!

Now that you have worked on 15 recipes,
it's time to use your imagination and get creative.
You can take ideas from the recipes you have already worked on
or think up something completely new. Let's get started:

What do I want to make:

- -

- -

What ingredients do I need:

What tools do I need:

What are the instructions:

Let's give it a name:

- - - - - - - - - - - - - - - - - -

draw a picture of the recipe:

Made in the USA
Middletown, DE
17 March 2017